Freedom in the Unknown

by

Sonja J. Miley

DORRANCE PUBLISHING CO., INC.
PITTSBURGH, PENNSYLVANIA 15222

ISBN: 978-1-4349-0351-8

Printed in the United States of America

First Printing

For more information or to order additional books,
please contact:
Dorrance Publishing Co., Inc.
701 Smithfield Street
Pittsburgh, Pennsylvania 15222
U.S.A.
1-800-788-7654
www.dorrancebookstore.com

This book is dedicated to KMM. Your wisdom, guidance, support, and love have felt like a cool drink of water for my thirsty soul. I am so very grateful.

Foreword to
Freedom in the Unknown by Sonja J. Miley

The creation of this book was a liberating process. During my four years of training at the Barbara Brennan School of Healing Europe, I was constantly intrigued and amazed at how the work within each Distance Learning Module (DLM) homework assignment perfectly matched the lesson I was learning in that period of my life. Somehow each DLM was synchronized to support me through the various life issues I was facing as I explored the depths of my interior landscape. This process was teaching me to let go of control and step with greater and greater confidence, excitement, and joy into the unknown. Every inch of introspection challenged me to move into the dark places within myself held in fear. As if guided by a helping hand, day-to-day occurrences seemed to act as a mirror into my life, reflecting externally where I had potential for growth. Why wouldn't the last piece of my last DLM assignment of my final year at BBSHE be any different? Interestingly, throughout the first three years of school, I knew exactly what I wanted to do for each creative arts project. So strong was this knowing that sometimes the creative pulse began the summer before the school year started. One can imagine my surprise when year four rolled around as did the months into the school year and nothing—zilch, zip, zero inspiration! I couldn't connect to a single project for creative arts. I had several ideas, but they didn't feel right and never amounted to anything. When presenting for creative arts, it was always extremely important that each project was closely linked to the theme of the school year and linked to what I was going through in that particular year. Not having an idea for a project terrified me. Am I going to fail? What is wrong with me? Why can't I be like everyone else? The self-judgments hit me with the force and persistence of waves crashing to the shore. Not having an idea bothered me so much that

I discussed my feelings with friends and colleagues. I even meditated on my project, clearing my mind for nothing else but a seed of something to appear. Still nothing. Incredulously, I began to notice how life was mirroring a valuable lesson through my situation. I was being challenged to let go and to live with *not* knowing. As I worked with this new concept of letting go of control, of knowing the outcome, I slowly began to relax. To my surprise, I started to enjoy the freedom I felt living in this place of the unknown. The more I didn't have a project, the more I trusted that an idea would emerge even if at the last minute. When friends asked, "What are you doing for your creative arts project?" I confidently and excitedly told them, "I don't know yet." The liberation I felt was incredible. To simply trust the process felt like being freed from self-imposed chains holding me separate from happiness, joy, and limitless possibilities. Much of my life I thought I needed to control everything in order to feel safe. But now I was learning to let go of a plan, dive into the unknown, and trust myself and the process. Always supported by life, the lessons reinforcing this were coming thick and fast. Finally, three weeks before the due date of our creative arts project, I remembered a poem I "channeled" a few months previous while in a meditative state (free-flow writing from a relaxed state). I liked the poem very much, and I remembered how incredible it felt to watch my pencil move and create words on my paper over which I had no control. Finally I had an idea to use my poem, but now I was struggling to formulate an idea about how to use it! My very wise and very patient teacher asked why I didn't simply use my poem. I couldn't possibly use my poem. "That's cheating," I replied hastily. When my teacher gently pushed a little further and asked why I felt it was cheating, I responded again by saying because it was too easy, so effortless. Shouldn't I sweat over my creation? Shouldn't it be difficult and fraught with struggle? Then it hit me like a stack of bricks tumbling down from one mighty blow of a wrecking ball. Of course I can use my poem as my project! It came from me and from the unmanifest within me. Isn't creation a process? In fact, isn't the process more important than the end result in many cases? Shortly after this moment of profound realization, I turned to my last reading assignment of my four-year BBSHE training and read the following passage from *Light Emerging* by Dr. Barbara Brennan. "The creative process or pulse of life has four phases. First is the stillness of the empty void deep within the core star. This is a point of stasis. Most of us do not give enough time for the stasis part of our creative wave. There are two phases in the stasis part of the creative wave: the part before expansion, when we are contracted and merged within our deepest self, and the part after expansion, when we are expanded and merged with another. In the first, we need quiet time alone to integrate who we are with what we have created in the past. We need to be alone to meet ourselves, to be with ourselves without doing anything. This time of centering is a time of gathering power without doing anything."

This book was submitted as my creative arts project in March 2008. There really is profound freedom living in the unknown.

Sonja J. Miley

The story unfolds like the whisper of the wind blowing against my face in the midst of a storm.

The storm within.

I write to save my life.

It is an act of self-preservation,

of completeness.

To expel the innermost nuances of my soul is a blessing beholden to me.

I write to capture the moment.

I write to let it all pass.

Over the hills
of my desire
I open
to the
energy
flowing
through
me.

Allowing what come, what may:

nothing more,

nothing less.

Allowing the emptiness, the nothingness to unfold, within and without.

Can we be nothing together?

No-thing?

Can we be our truth in unison,

without conflict,

without persecution,

without fear?

I unfold upon you and let go the images of my long-held fear.

I can see me clearly.

I can feel you and your breath.

Breathe with
me, my brother,

for I am the
butterfly upon
your cheek.

Hold me, my sister, for my heart is in your hands.

The Beginning . . .

Index

Sonja's photos from travel around the world:

1. Page 1, photo: Raindrop Window and Double Rainbow; Bad Neuanahr, Germany; 10 November 2007.
2. Page 3, photo: Climbing Mountain; Ben Nevis, Scotland; July 2004.
3. Page 4, photo: Sunrise over Lake; Mondsee, Austria; 2004.
4. Page 5, photos: Peace Wall; Belfast, Northern Ireland; July 1998.
5. Page 6, photo: Painted Mural on Mountain Representing the Evolution of Native Life; Vinales Valley, Cuba (100 miles west of Havana); July 2004.
6. Page 7, photo: Sunset; Greenwich, Connecticut, USA; August 2002.
7. Page 8, photo: Little Mermaid; Copenhagen, Denmark; 2003.
8. Page 9, photos: Strangers Connecting with Heart (Sonja and young woman from Tatog tribe); Lake Eyasi, Tanzania, Africa; June 1997.
9. Page 10, photo: Hindu Temple; Shimla, India; March 2007.
10. Page 11, photo: Graffiti from Orange Revolution (Tak! means Yes!); Kiev, Ukraine; May 2005.
11. Page 12, photos: Red Square; Moscow, Russia; April 2003.
12. Page 13, photo: Spice Bazaar; Istanbul, Turkey; December 2007.
13. Page 14, photo: Wooden Bridge; Kwa Mhlanga District, near Pretoria, South Africa; February 2008.
14. Page 15, photo: Table Mountain; Cape Town, South Africa; December 2002.
15. Page 16, photo: Making Friends with Fenne; Kwa Mhlanga District, near Pretoria, South Africa; February 2008.
16. Page 17, photo: Butterfly; Kwa Mhlanga District, near Pretoria, South Africa; February 2008.
17. Page 18, photo: Heart in Hand; London, England; March 2008.